WHO IS CUTER?

Baby Bat or Baby Opossum?

by Mari Schuh

BLASTOFF! READERS 1

BLASTOFF! READERS, AN IMPRINT OF BELLWETHER MEDIA BY FLUTTERBEE

Blastoff! Readers are carefully developed by literacy experts to build reading stamina and move students toward fluency by combining standards-based content with developmentally appropriate text.

LEVELS

Level 1 provides the most support through repetition of high-frequency words, light text, predictable sentence patterns, and strong visual support.

Level 2 offers early readers a bit more challenge through varied sentences, increased text load, and text-supportive special features.

Level 3 advances early-fluent readers toward fluency through increased text load, less reliance on photos, advancing concepts, longer sentences, and more complex special features.

★ **Blastoff! Universe**

This edition first published in 2027 by Bellwether Media, Inc.

For information regarding permission, write to Bellwether Media, Inc., Attention: Permissions Department, 3500 American Blvd W, Suite 150, Bloomington, MN 55431.

Library of Congress Cataloging-in-Publication Data is available at www.loc.gov or upon request from the publisher.

ISBN: 9798898800239 (hardcover)
ISBN: 9798898801472 (ebook)

Editor: Rachael Barnes Designer: Jennifer Bowyer

Printed in the United States of America, North Mankato, MN.

Table of Contents

Pups and Joeys!

Baby bats are called pups. Baby opossums are called joeys.

joeys
pup

Both babies are **nocturnal**. They stay close to mom.

mom flying with her pup

Legs and Wings

Pups have wings.
Joeys have
four short legs.

wing
legs

Joeys have white, gray, and black fur. Pup bodies have fur. But their wings are **bare**.

bare
wing
fur

Joeys have pointy **snouts**. Pup snouts are much shorter.

snout

Growing Up

Pups are often born one at a time. Joeys are born in **litters**.

litter

Pups hang upside down. They hang in caves and in trees. Joeys climb on mom's back.

Joeys learn to climb trees. Pups learn to fly. Who is cuter?

pup

Who Is Cuter?

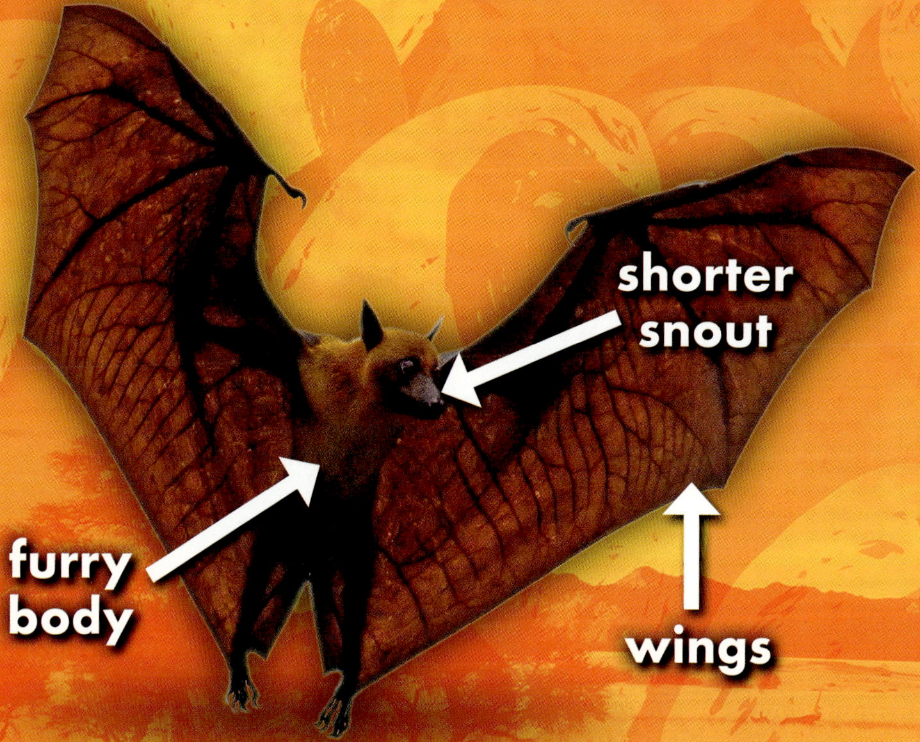

Baby Bat

Who is your pick? Vote at BellwetherMedia.com

Baby Opossum

Glossary

bare

not covered

litters

groups of baby animals born at the same time

nocturnal

active at night

snouts

the noses and mouths of some animals

To Learn More

AT THE LIBRARY

Deniston, Natalie. *Opossums.* Minneapolis, Minn.: Jump!, 2025.

Richmond, Marley. *Night Flight.* North Mankato, Minn.: Picture Window Books, 2026.

Scheffer, Janie. *Brown Bats.* Minneapolis, Minn.: Bellwether Media, 2026.

ON THE WEB

FACTSURFER

Factsurfer.com gives you a safe, fun way to find more information.

1. Go to www.factsurfer.com.
2. Enter "baby bat or baby opossum" into the search box and click .
3. Select your book cover to see a list of related content.

Index

The images in this book are reproduced through the courtesy of: sorind72, front cover (bat), pp. 16-17; rthoma, front cover (opossum); Gregory Escande, p. 3 (bat); Robert Eastman, p. 3 (meerkat); Image Source Limited/ Thomas Kitchin & Victoria Hurst/ Alamy, pp. 4-5, 17, 21 (climbs on mom); Hans Neleman/ Getty Images, pp. 5, 20 (born one at a time); Ivan Kuzmin, pp. 6-7; Tommy Daynjer, p. 7; Doug Gimesy, pp. 8-9, 19, 22 (snouts); Joe Austin Photography/ Alamy, p. 9; Jay Ondreicka, pp. 10-11; Genevieve Vallee/ Alamy, pp. 11, 22 (bare); Jens_Bee, pp. 12-13; Francisco J. de Anda, p. 13; Abril, pp. 14-15, 22 (litters); Tierfotoagentur / Fotofeeling/ Alamy, p. 15; imageBROKER/R. Wittek/ Alamy, pp. 18-19; aDam Wildlife, p. 20 (main bat); Nature Picture Library/ Steven David Miller/ Alamy, p. 20 (hangs upside down); Ivan Kuzmin/ Alamy, p. 20 (learns to fly); Tony Wear, p. 21 (main opossum); Heiko Kiera, p. 21 (born in a litter); stanley45, p. 21 (learns to climb trees); Francisco J. de Anda, p. 22 (nocturnal).